Biographies

Zoë Aldrich (Albine)
Theatre includes: *Her Naked ...*
Baby (Hampstead Theatre), *7 ...*
Palace), *Macbeth, The Change ...*
(Shakespeare at the Tobacco Factory, Bristol and Barbican), *Peter Pan*
(Birmingham Rep), *Much Ado About Nothing* (Cheek by Jowl), *Second
From Last in the Sack Race, The Rover* and *An Ideal Husband* (Salisbury
Playhouse), *The Broken Heart* (Lyric Hammersmith), *The House of
Bernada Alba* (Gate Theatre). TV includes: *Doctors, Hollyoaks, Silent
Witness* and *The Knock*. Radio: *Travels in West Africa* (Radio 4 Book of
the Week).

Jude Akuwudike (Burrhus)
Jude trained at RADA. Recent theatre includes *The Faith Machine* (Royal
Court), *Great Expectations* (English Touring Theatre), *Othello* (Glasgow
Citizens Theatre), *Iya-Ile* (Tiata Fahodzi/Soho Theatre), *Walking
Waterfall* (Tiata Delights '08, Almeida Theatre), *The Resistable Rise of
Arturo Uri* (Lyric Hammersmith), *God in Ruins* (Soho Theatre), *Macbeth
and Macbett* (RSC), *The Overwhelming, Edmond* and *Henry V* (National
Theatre) and *Pericles* (Globe). On television, Jude recently starred in the
UK version of *Law & Order,* Joe Penhall's *Moses Jones* and *The #1 Ladies
Detective Agency* (BBC). Film includes *The Tempest, Touched By A
Stranger, Whisper the Way of the Child, Sahara* and *A World Apart*.

Christopher Colquhoun (Narcissus)
Trained at RADA. Theatre includes *Happy Now?* (Hull Truck); *Five Guys
Named Moe* (Theatre Royal Stratford East and the Edinburgh
International Festival); *Troilus and Cressida* (Globe); *Macbeth* (Royal
Exchange Manchester), nominated for Best Actor in a Supporting Role
at the Manchester Evening News Theatre Awards; *The Thief of Baghdad*
(Royal Opera House); *Three Sisters* (Royal Exchange Manchester);
Saint Joan (National Theatre); *Comedy of Errors* (RSC); *Simply Heavenly*
(Trafalgar Studios); *Ain't Misbehavin'* (Derby Playhouse); *Blues in the
Night* (Birmingham Rep); *Snake in the Fridge, The Way of the World*
(Royal Exchange, Manchester); *Angels in America* (Crucible Theatre,
Sheffield); and *Moby Dick, King Lear, The Tempest, The Merchant of
Venice* (RSC). Despite his significant theatre credits, Chris is probably
still most recognisable as Dr. Simon Kaminski from Casualty. Most
recently, he completed filming on the American Television Series,
Missing. Other Television credits include: *Coronation Street* (ITV Granada);

Wire in the Blood (Carnival Films); *Belonging* (BBC); *North Square* (YTV); *Silent Witness* (BBC); *London Bridge* (Carlton); *Band of Gold* (Thames); *Shakespeare Shorts* (BBC) and *The Bill* (Talkback Thames).

Matthew Needham (Nero)
Matthew trained at LAMDA. Theatre includes *Double Feature* (National Theatre, dir. Lindsay Turner), *Shades* (Royal Court), *The Grapes of Wrath* and *Bingo* (Chichester Festival Theatre). TV includes *Monroe*, *Sherlock* and *Casualty*.

Sian Thomas (Agrippina)
Sian's theatre credits include *Who's afraid of Virginia Woolf* (Sheffield Crucible); *The Persians* (NTW); *The Goat* (Traverse, Best Actress - Critics' Award for Theatre in Scotland); *Spring Awakenings* (Lyric Hammersmith/ West End); *Small Craft Warning* (Arcola Theatre); *Fram* (National Theatre); *Ghosts* (Bristol Old Vic); *The Glass Room* (Hampstead Theatre); *Macbeth* and *Hamlet* (RSC/Albery Theatre); *The Prince* (Apollo/Tricycle, Best Actress - What's On Stage Award); *Up For Grabs* (Sonia Friedman - Olivier Award Nominated); *Push Up* (Royal Court); *Feelgood* (Hampstead/ Garrick Theatre); *House and Garden, Sleep With Me, Richard II, The Mountain Goats, Square Rounds, The Misanthrope, Country Mania* (Olivier Award Nomination, Best Comedy Performance), *The Wandering Jew* and *The Way Of The World* (National Theatre); *King Lear, Richard III, Taming of the Shrew, Happy End* (RSC) and *Delicate Balance* (Theatre Royal Haymarket). Her television credits include *The Royal Bodyguard, Thinspiration, Half Broken Things, Lewis, Ruby in the Smoke, Holby City, Vincent, The Last Detective and The Worst Week Of My Life* and *Inspector Morse*. Her film credits include *Harry Potter and the Half Blood Prince*, Harry *Potter and the Order of the Phoenix, Perfume* and *Vanity Fair*.

Alexander Vlahos (Britannicus)
Alexander graduated from The Royal Welsh College of Music and Drama in 2009. Theatre credits include: *Emperor and Galilean* (National Theatre), *Theatre Ashes* (IronBark at Latitude Festival), *Present: Tense* (Nabakov at Watford Palace Theatre), *Hamlet* (Sheffield Crucible), *Cardiff Assembly* (National Theatre Wales), *The Elsinore Project* (Volcano) and *Café Cariad* (National Youth Theatre Wales). Television includes the regular character of Tom Evans in *The Indian Doctor* (BBC) which won Best Daytime Drama at the RTS awards 2010, *Pentalar* (S4C), *The Tower (*Uzong Films), Lewis Cutler in 5 episodes of a self contained storyline in *Doctors* (BBC), *Crash* (BBC Wales), *Herio'r Draig* (S4C), *A Dwi Mor Hapus* (S4C), *Thick Cut* (BBC Wales), *Pobol Y Cwm* (BBC Wales), *Y Meicrosgop Hud* (S4C). He is soon to be seen in the feature film *Truth or Dare*.

Hara Yannas (Junia)
Hara graduated from LAMDA in 2009. Theatre includes *Pericles* (Open Air Theatre, Regent's Park), *Uncle Vanya* (Arcola Theatre/Belgrade Theatre, Coventry), *it felt empty when the heart went at first but it is alright now* (Arcola Theatre/Clean Break), *A Midsummer Night's Dream* (Shakespeare's Globe and Tour), *Tales Of The Harrow Road* (Soho Theatre), *Scrooge* (National Tour). Television includes *Holby City* (BBC).

•

Jean Racine
Jean Racine was born on 22 December 1639 in Ferté-Milon, France. At the age of ten he entered the Petites Ecoles of Port Royal, an educational establishment heavily influenced by Jansenism. He moved to Paris in 1658 where he completed his studies. In 1664–5 two plays, *La Thébaïde* and *Alexandre le Grand*, were performed by Molière's company at the Théâtre du Palais-Royal, Paris. They were followed by *Andromaque* (1667), *Les Plaideurs* (1668), *Britannicus* (1669), *Bérénice* (1670), *Bajazet* (1672), *Mithridate* (1673), *Iphigénie* (1674) and *Phèdre* (1677). In 1678, he stopped writing for the theatre and became the biographer of Louis XIV. He wrote only two other plays before his death in 1699, both on Biblical subjects. *Britannicus* was initially received with hostility, closing after just seven performances in 1669; but it was revived a year later – largely thanks to the enthusiasm of Louis XIV – and has remained Racine's second-most produced work in France ever since.

Timberlake Wertenbaker (Playwright)
Grew up in the Basque Country and lives in London. Her plays include for the Royal Court: *Our Country's Good*, *The Grace of Mary Traverse*, *Three Birds Alighting on a Field*, *The Break of Day* and *Credible Witness*. Among her other works are *The Love of the Nightingale* (RSC), *Galileo's Daughter* (Theatre Royal, Bath), *The Ash Girl* (Birmingham Rep), *After Darwin* (Hampstead Theatre) and *The Line* (Arcola Theatre) Translations and adaptations include Sophocles' *Theban Plays* (RSC), Euripides' *Hecuba* (ACT, San Francisco), Eduardo de Filippo's *Filumena* (Piccadilly), Gabriela Preissova's *Jenufa* (Arcola), Sophocles' *Elektra* (Getty), Racine's *Phèdre* (Shakespeare Festival, Stratford, Ontario.) Opera includes *The Love of the Nightingale*, music by Richard Mills (Perth International Arts Festival 2006 and Sydney Opera House 2011). Timberlake is joint Artistic Director of Natural Perspective.

Irina Brown (Director)
Born and educated in St Petersburg. Joint Artistic Director of Natural Perspective Theatre Company. Artistic Director of the Tron Theatre,

Glasgow (1996-2000). Recent theatre and opera credits include: *War and Peace at the Circus* (adaptor/ director - Giffords Circus); *Desire Lines* by Ian Rowlands (Sherman Cymru); Prokofiev's *War and Peace* (RSAMD/ Scottish Opera); *Gamblers* (LPO, Royal Festival Hall); *The Letter* (5:15 Scottish Opera); *The Importance of Being Earnest* (Open Air Theatre, Regents Park); *Bird of Night* by Dominique Le Gendre (Royal Opera House); *Three Tall Women* (Oxford Playhouse/ tour); *The Vagina Monologues* (London's West End/national tour); *Further than the Furthest Thing* (National Theatre/ Tron); Andrei Tarkovsky's *Boris Godunov* (ROH/ Monte Carlo). Other credits: *The Cosmonaut's Last Message to the Woman He Once Loved in the Former Soviet Union* (Tron, Glasgow); *The Sound of Music* (WYP); *Our Country's Good* (Moscow).

Chloe Lamford (Designer)
Chloe trained at Wimbledon School of Art. She won Best Design at the 2007 TMA awards. Recent theatre includes: *Knives In Hens* (National Theatre Scotland), *Disco Pigs, Sus* (Young Vic), *On The Record* (Arcola Theatre), *Ghost Story* (Sky Arts), *My Romantic History* (Bush Theatre), *Joseph K, The Kreutzer Sonata* (Gate Theatre), *Songs From A Hotel Bedroom* (ROH2), *It Felt Empty...* (Clean Break), *This Wide Night* (Soho Theatre). Opera includes *The Magic Flute* (ETO), *War and Peace* (Scottish Opera), *Cunning Little Vixen, Orpheus in the Underworld* (Royal College Music), *La Calisto* (Early Opera Company).

Simon Mills (Lighting Designer)
Simon Mills has designed lighting for opera, theatre, film and dance in 20+ countries. He has lit productions varying in size from the Bush Theatre to Roman amphitheatres and football stadia. In addition he designs lighting for architectural practices, ecclesiastic buildings, galleries and domestic interiors. He also consults on theatre design.

Pippa Ailion (Casting Director)
Pippa has cast over 120 productions for West End, UK, US and Europe. Current West End: *Million Dollar Quartet*; *Legally Blonde*; *Wicked*; *Billy Elliot*; *The Lion King*; *We Will Rock You* (and UK tour). Recent: *Decade* (Headlong); *Top Hat* (UK tour); *The Go Between* (WYP & tour); *Sweeney Todd* (Chichester); *Rocky Horror Show* (Germany); *Waiting For Godot* (WYP); *The Wiz* (Birmingham/WYP); *Lord of the Flies, Into the Woods, The Importance of Being Earnest* (Regent's Park); *Love Story* (Duchess & Chichester); *Fela!* (NT); *Spring Awakening; Peter Pan* (O2 & USA tour); *The Fairy Queen* (New York Glyndebourne). Associates: Casting Director - James Hopson. Casting Co-Ordinator - Natalie Gallacher.

Sarah Llewellyn (Composer)
Trained at GSMD. Credits include: Giffords Circus (UK tours) *War and Peace, Yasmine a Musical* & *Caravan*. Fairbanks Shakespeare Theatre (Alaska): *Much Ado About Nothing, Antony and Cleopatra, Henry V.* Anchovy Pictures: *Oscar and Jim.* Red Shift Theatre: *Much Ado About Nothing* (UK Tour) & *The Fall of Man* (Edinburgh Fringe & UK tour). Charlotte Jones' *Airswimming* (Arcola Istanbul), Charlotte Delbo's *Who Will Carry the Word* (Courtyard Theatre London), Howard Brenton's *Weapons of Happiness* (Finborough), Keith Dewhurst's *King Arthur* (Arcola London). Clarity Productions: Documentary *Contempt of Conscience, Hansel and Gretel* (Windsor), *Caligari* (Unity Liverpool & Music Rooms Mayfair London), *Misery* (The Brindley Runcorn) & *Wall Talks* (The Blade Factory, Liverpool). Sarah is founder and director of music company tonal.

Marcin Rudy (Movement Director)
Marcin Rudy is a movement director, actor and teacher. Since the year 2000 he has been collaborating with the multi-award winning physical theatre company Song of the Goat Theatre (Poland) as a performer/ deviser. He has performed in 22 countries on 5 continents, at venues including Barbican, Sydney Opera House, Taipei National Theatre, La MaMa New York. His work as a movement director includes various major shows in Italy and UK.

Barbara Houseman (Voice work)
Production Voice Coach includes: *Playboy of the Western World* (Old Vic); *Government Inspector* (Young Vic); *All's Well That Ends Well* (Globe); *Design for Living* (Old Vic); '09, '10, '11 seasons at Regent's Park Theatre; *Misanthrope* (Comedy). Personal Voice Coach includes: Jude Law, *Hamlet, Anna Christie*; Daniel Radcliffe, *Equus*; Kenneth Branagh, *Richard III*. Associate Director – voice/text: *Romeo and Juliet* (Naples Festival '10); *Comedy of Errors, More Grimm Tales* (Young Vic). Voice/Text Coach, Royal Shakespeare Company '91-'97 includes: *Macbeth* (Derek Jacobi); *Hamlet* (Kenneth Branagh); *Richard III* (Simon Russell Beale); *A Midsummer Night's Dream* (Alex Jennings).

John Walton (Assistant Director)
John trained at the Ecole Philippe Gaullier. His directors credits include: *Yoroboshi* by Yukio Mishima (New Wimbledon Studio); *Dr Brown Because* (Edinburgh Fringe / Soho Theatre); *Marcello al Dente Relives a Catastrophic Moment in His Life* (Edinburgh Fringe); *Potato - A Show That Will Save the World* (Edinburgh Fringe and European Tour); *A Little*

Princess by Vera Morris and Bill Francoeur after Frances Hodgson Burnett (Hedgerow Theatre, Pennsylvania); *Blasted* by Sarah Kane (Old Fire Station, Oxford); *The Decision* by Bertold Brecht (Burton-Taylor Theatre, Oxford).

Shaz McGee (Production Manager)
Shaz studied at The University of Kent from where she went on to join Ra Ra Zoo, a circus company with whom she toured the world. Other theatre credits include The National Theatre, Trestle Theatre Company, The Circus Space, Momentary Fusion and The Gandini Juggling Project. She is currently Technical Director at The Tricycle Theatre.

Paul Kizintas (Production Manager and Sound Designer)
Paul has worked on numerous productions since 2000. This has been a varied mix of dance, music and theatre. A small selection includes: *The Great Game: Afghanistan* (Tricycle), Spill Festival of performance (Pacitti company – Shunt Vaults), *How Long is Never: Darfur – a response* (Sound design, Tricycle), *Called to Account* (Sound design, Tricycle), *The Vegemite Tales* (production engineer, Itchy feet theatre). In addition Paul has worked as an FOH engineer on a number of shows and productions in venues ranging from St Pancras Old Church to Sadler's Wells.

Julia Blom (Stage Manager)
Julia has a background in event and project management in the Netherlands. In London, she has worked at Sadler's Wells and the Barbican and has been a Venue Stage Manager for Pleasance Edinburgh for the last three years. Julia's stage management credits include *Macbeth* (Broadway Theatre), *Miss Julie* (Arcola Theatre), *Sister Of* (Nursery Festival), *Secret Boulevard* (Courtyard Theatre), *MEAT* (The Albany & Lion and Unicorn), *Oh, To Be in England* (Finborough Theatre), *Fragments* (Riverside Studios) and *Tender Napalm* (Southwark Playhouse). She has also worked on several festivals at the Royal Albert Hall and Sadler's Wells, including Breakin' Convention 09 and 10.

Scarlett Alexander (Deputy Stage Manager)
Scarlett studied French Language and Civilisation at the Sorbonne in Paris. She has just finished a five months tour of *War and Peace at the Circus* (Giffords Circus) directed by Irina Brown. During rehearsals she was an Assistant to the Director and to the Choreographer, and on tour became Assistant Stage Manger, with responsibilities which included operating the sound and lighting as well as performing Front of House duties.

Amy Gunn (Assistant Stage Manager)
After graduating from The University of Sheffield in 2010, Amy has worked as crew at Edinburgh and Brighton Fringes and with professional companies in Bradford and London. Her work has included Assistant Stage Manager for *The Mill: City of Dreams*, produced by Freedom Studios and Stage Manager for *The Story Project 3* at Southwark Playhouse. Amy also works freelance as a director, participating in new writing events in addition to stage management work.

Ben Monks (Producer for Natural Perspective)
Ben first worked with Natural Perspective as fundraising manager on *Jenufa*. He runs the production company Supporting Wall with Will Young, where recent credits include Philip Ridley's *Tender Napalm* (Southwark Playhouse), 2010 JMK award-winner *The Jewish Wife* (BAC), *Moonfleece* (London & tour), the forthcoming *Shallow Slumber* (Soho Theatre), and UK and international tours of Rachel Rose Reid's *I'm Hans Christian Andersen* and Frauke Requardt's *Episode*. Ben produced YouTube sensation *Gap Yah* for The Unexpected Items in 2010, and is a previous recipient of the SOLT/TMA Stage One Bursary and nominee for Best Producer at the OffWestEnd 'Offie' Awards. He is Creative Producer at the Tristan Bates Theatre, Covent Garden.

We would like to thank the Tricycle Theatre, Niamh Dowling, Dr Michael Hawcroft, Gregory Nash, Alexander Zeldin, Jools Osborne, Royal College of Music; and the actors who took part in the development workshop: Gethin Anthony, Tom Burke, Jay Choi, Monica Dolan, Mark Letheren and Lauren O'Neil.

WILTON'S

THE CITY'S HIDDEN STAGE

Wilton's is the world's oldest surviving Grand Music Hall and London's best kept secret. This stunning and atmospheric building is home to an exciting programme of diverse and distinct entertainment including theatre, music, comedy, cinema and cabaret.

The Hall has a colourful and rich history. It was built in 1858 by John Wilton who had the vision to create a Grand Music Hall. It was a success from the start and some of the greatest Music Hall stars performed such as Champagne Charlie and Arthur Lloyd. Some historians even argue that Britain's first Can Can was seen on Wilton's stage!

By the 1880s new fire regulations marked the demise of its use and the hall closed. It was then purchased by a local Wesleyan Mission and used until the 1950s as a Methodist Mission, witnessing major moments in history such as the Docker's Strike of 1889, the Battle of Cable Street in 1936 and two World Wars. When the Methodists left, Wilton's became derelict, unstable and under threat.

The building's fortunes have now changed and over the past few years it has been lovingly and sensitively brought to life by the Wilton's Music Hall Trust. A Capital Project is underway to conserve and protect the structure and fabric of the building, while the team continue to produce an imaginative array of live events that celebrate its past yet define a vibrant future.

Support Wilton's

Wilton's is a charity and receives no public funding. It uses an entrepreneurial spirit to survive and generates income from location hire, box office revenue, fundraising and bar sales. We would like to thank our generous supporters listed below as well as all of our Friends and volunteers. To find out more about becoming a Friend or Patron or donating to our Capital Project please call 020 7702 9555 or go to wiltons.org.uk.

PATRONS

JOHN WILTON'S INNER CIRCLE
Henry Lewis
Mark & Liza Loveday
Stephen & Linda Simpson
Hilary & Stuart Williams

CAN CAN DANCER
Jonathan Kitchen

CHAMPAGNE CHARLIE
Anonymous
Clyde Cooper
John Crisp
David Crook
Ruth Finch
Joachim Fleury
Daniel Friel
Dr & Mrs Gayner
A. J. S. Gunn
Mike Kavanagh
George Law
Joan Major
George & Ann Marsh
Mr & Mrs David Pennock
Rev. David Rogers
Jon & NoraLee Sedmak
David & Sheila Suchet & Friends
Jan & Michael Topham

FRIENDS

SHILLING BOXES
Christine Cromwell-Ahrens
Alexandra Gammie
Mr & Mrs Nicholas Harris
The LeBrocq Family Jersey
David Pike
John & Stephanie Riley

EIGHTPENNY STALLS
Mr & Mrs Sherban Cantacuzino
Adrian Clarke
Amanda Dixon
Fredo Donnelly & Mike Richardson
Mr & Mrs Elliott Schwartz

Sir Stuart Ethrington
Martin Gordon
Colin & Felicity Luke
Judith Morgan
Michael O'Callaghan
Lord and Lady Phillimore
Mark Phillippo
David Poole
Tessa Pye
Gavin Ralston
Bruce Rowling
Carolyn Saunders
Dasha Shenkman
John Wright

CORPORATES

Astell Scientific
Brand Evolution
Carlsberg
Cluttons
The Corner Shop PR
Gilchrist and Soames
Latham and Watkins LLP
Radisson Edwardian (Official Hotel Sponsor)
Waitrose

TRUSTS AND FOUNDATIONS

The Batchworth Trust
The Bernarr Rainbow Foundation
The Coutts Charitable Trust
The Noël Coward Foundation
The Foundation for Sport and the Arts
Colin and Anna Frizzell Charitable Trust
The Anthony Hornby Trust
The Loveday Foundation
The National Trust
News International Staff Association
Charities Committee
The Stuart and Hilary Williams Charitable Foundation

IN-KIND SUPPORT
Alexandra Park & Palace Charitable Trust
Andrew Gorman
Eddy Smith

Jean Racine
Britannicus

translated and adapted by
TIMBERLAKE WERTENBAKER

faber and faber

First published in 2011
by Faber and Faber Limited
74–77 Great Russell Street
London WC1B 3DA

Typeset by Country Setting, Kingsdown, Kent CT14 8ES
Printed and bound by CPI Group (UK) Ltd, Croydon CR0 4YY

A CIP record for this book
is available from the British Library

ISBN 978–0–571–28397–2

2 4 6 8 10 9 7 5 3 1

Characters

in order of appearance

Agrippina
widow of the Emperor Claudius
and Nero's mother

Albine
Agrippina's confidante

Burrhus
Nero's tutor and adviser

Britannicus
Claudius's son by his first wife

Narcissus
Britannicus's tutor

Nero
Emperor and son of Agrippina

Junia
betrothed to Britannicus

Rome, Nero's palace

Act One

Agrippina, Albine.

Albine

So – while Nero still wallows in his sleep
you wait here meekly for him to emerge?
Must you wander alone through the palace?
You – Nero's mother – and stand by his door?
Go back, go back now, return to your rooms.

Agrippina

No, Albine, there isn't a moment to lose –
I have to wait for him here. The torment
he inflicts on me keeps me occupied.
What I foresaw so clearly has happened:
Nero has turned against Britannicus.
Impetuous Nero has lost all restraint:
bored with being loved, he wants to be feared.
Britannicus is in his way, Albine,
and each day I am myself less welcome.

Albine

How could that be? Didn't you give him life and
an empire he was not born to rule?
Didn't you disinherit Britannicus,
the true heir, and offer Rome to your son?
He owes everything to Agrippina –
he owes you his love –

Agrippina

He owes me his love.
If Nero's noble he'll obey this law
but if ungrateful, he'll turn against me.

5

Albine
> Ungrateful? But Nero's whole demeanour
> shows a heart obedient to his duty.
> For three years what has he done other than
> demonstrate he'll make a perfect emperor?
> A golden age seems to have returned here
> equal to the time the consuls governed.
> He's Rome's father. And Nero emerging
> has the virtues of Augustus aging.

Agrippina
> My interests don't blind me to his virtues.
> He's begun, true, where Augustus left off
> but I fear the future could wipe the past
> and he'll end the way Augustus began.
> I see through his mask, I read on his face
> the grim and savage pride of his lineage.
> Remember how many began as well:
> tyranny always promises good things.
> But – do I really care if Nero leaves
> behind him a model of virtue?
> I didn't place all that power in his hands
> for the sake of the senate and the people.
> Let him be, if he chooses, Rome's father
> but let him remember I'm his mother.
> What can we say about last night's action?
> He knows as well as anyone
> the love Britannicus feels for Junia.
> And this Nero, this virtuous Nero
> has Junia seized in the dark of the night.
> What does he want? Is it love? Is it hate?
> Does he only want to make them suffer?
> Or is he making mischief to punish me
> since he knows I've given them my support?

Albine
> I didn't know you supported them.

Agrippina

Indeed –
and I know that I alone caused their ruin,
that I tripped Britannicus as he climbed
to the throne that was his inheritance.
And Junia's brother, who loved Octavia,
took his life when I gave her to Nero.
I gave Nero all but I must control
the balance between them – so that one day
Britannicus can hold that same balance
between my power and that of my son.

Albine

What a plan!

Agrippina

I need a safe haven in the tempest.
Nero escapes me if I don't stop him.

Albine

So many precautions against a son?

Agrippina

If he fears me I don't have to fear him.

Albine

I wonder if your fears are well founded.
Whenever Rome gives Nero a title
he passes it on to Agrippina.
He gives you everything, he keeps nothing
and your name in Rome is as revered as his.
Octavia his wife is barely mentioned.
You carry all the emblems of power:
what more can you ask of his gratitude?

Agrippina

A little less display and much more trust.
My honours increase as my power wanes.
A long time has passed since a young Nero

directed the court's worship to me,
when he placed affairs of state in my hands
and the senate responded to my call,
when, veiled, invisible, always present
I was the all-powerful heart of Rome.
Nero wasn't yet drunk on his glory –
he was still uncertain of his power.
But I still remember that fateful day
when kings sent ambassadors to honour
and name him master of the universe –
I saw then Nero dazzled by his fame.
I went towards the throne to take my place
next to him. What plan prepared my disgrace?
As soon as Nero caught sight of me there
his face became suffused with displeasure:
it struck at my heart like a dark presage.
He got up, ran to embrace me and then,
covering his insult with false respect,
he guided me firmly away from the throne.
Since that dark day, Agrippina's power
moves fast and inexorably to its end.
I have only its shadow: the people
seek Burrhus, woo Seneca, ignore me.

Albine
Why feed on the venom that makes you ill?
If all these doubts are troubling your spirit,
speak to your son, make yourself clear.

Agrippina
Nero won't see me without others there –
in public, at an appointed hour,
I'm granted audience and his two masters
set his answers or dictate his silence.
But the more he flees the more I'll chase him.
I'll take advantage of his disarray –
I hear a noise, he's coming, let's go now:

8

I'll ask him the reason for this kidnap
and prise open what he hides in his heart.
But look, Burrhus has been here before me.

SCENE TWO

Agrippina, Burrhus, Albine.

Burrhus

On Nero's behalf I was to tell you
of an order that may have alarmed you,
but it is only a wise precaution
which he wishes you to understand.

Agrippina

Since it's his wish, let's go in, he'll tell me.

Burrhus

The Emperor is not available now:
The two consuls have preceded you here –
they came unseen, through a private door.
However, I could go back and ask him . . .

Agrippina

I won't interrupt such weighty secrets –
but would it be possible for us now
to speak about some matters truthfully?

Burrhus

Burrhus is a man who abhors all lies.

Agrippina

For how long will you hide Nero from me?
Must I go down on my knees to see him?
Did I help you rise above all others
so you could erect a wall between us?
Are you afraid to leave him to me?
Are you now competing with Seneca

to see who can make him forget me first?
Who asked you to teach him ingratitude?
Why do you try to rule Rome in his name?
You seem to treat me as your creature
but it's you I plucked from obscurity
when you languished in some Roman outpost.
I follow my ancestors to this throne:
daughter, wife and sister of your rulers.
Do you think that I made him an emperor
so you could impose your will on me?
Nero is not a child, can't he rule now?
How long must the Emperor fear you both?
Can he see nothing you haven't shown him?
If he needs models he has ancestors:
let him look to Tiberius, Augustus
or mirror my father Germanicus.
I may not claim a place as great as these
but there are still virtues I can teach him
and remind him that an emperor must keep
his distance and his trust from mere subjects.

Burrhus
My only intention in seeing you
was to excuse Nero's single action –
but since you have asked me to justify
not this action but the rest of his life,
I will answer with the freedom expected
of an old soldier who doesn't mask facts.
You asked me to look after Nero's youth.
I admit that and I never forget.
But when did I promise to betray him?
Make him an emperor who only says yes?
You are not the one I answer to now.
He's no longer your son but Rome's master
and I take my orders from the empire,
which will rise or fall by his governance.
If he was to be brought up ignorant

why bother with Seneca or with me?
The court of Claudius was fertile in slaves.
You could have found a thousand volunteers
vying for the honour to degrade him
and keep him an infant until old age.
What makes you so unhappy? You're revered.
When they swear by the Emperor, they name you.
It's true that Nero no longer places
the empire at your feet, in your court.
But should he do that? Must his gratitude
always show itself in his dependence?
Must a timid Nero, always humble,
have of an emperor no more than the name?
Let me say it now: Rome is proud of him.
Rome, so long in the hands of favourites,
only now feels the lifting of its yoke
and breathes in the freedom of Nero's reign.
Our ancient virtue seems restored to us –
the empire is no longer a toy.
Nero takes the advice of his soldiers
and the deserts once full of senators
are peopled now by those who denounced them.
Does it matter if he listens to us
as long as during a flourishing reign,
Rome remains free and Nero powerful?
But Nero can justify his own rule.
I obey, I don't pretend to teach him.
He must indeed learn from his forebears, but
if he imitates himself he'll do well:
happy if, with all his virtues preserved,
he remains, down the years, just as he is.

Agrippina

I see you don't really trust the future
since you think Nero will fail without you.
Well now, if you're so pleased with your results,
and you can extol his many virtues,

tell us on what grounds, using brute force,
Nero has ordered Junia's kidnap?
What is she accused of? With what attempt
did she become so suddenly Rome's foe?
She who until now was raised without pride,
who never saw Nero before this raid –
who might have deemed it the greatest blessing
had she never set eyes on him at all?

Burrhus

She is not suspected of any crime
nor has Nero condemned her until now.
She is in her ancestral palace here,
she's seen nothing that might make her afraid.
But you know her inheritance brings rights
that could make of a husband a rebel
and that Nero's blood must only be joined
to those whom Nero has chosen himself.
Would you yourself not find it unusual
if Nero had no say in her marriage?

Agrippina

So: Nero uses your voice to tell me
that I've been deceiving Britannicus.
I wanted to console him for his plight
and encouraged him to trust in this love.
Nero now wants to prove to all Romans
that Agrippina's words have no power.
Rome has too long believed in my status
and with this insult he now sets Rome right
and lets the whole world learn with new terror
not to confuse my son with the Emperor.
He can do that, but let me remind him
that he needs to strengthen his empire
before he reduces me to the need
of testing my small powers against his.
He could undermine his authority
if he tried to pit his name against mine.

Burrhus

Must you always question Nero's respect?
Did the Emperor say you are plotting
and taking the side of Britannicus?
Will you now support Nero's enemies
and seek a reason to find fault with him?
Must you always, when you hear about him,
be ready to divide the empire?
Could you not cease to act as a censor
and be instead the indulgent mother,
accept some distance from him without rage
and not prompt the court to beware of you?

Agrippina

Who will be interested in my support
when Nero himself destroys my power?
When he will not even let me near him,
when Burrhus dares to keep me from his door?

Burrhus

It seems that my plain speaking has annoyed you.
Pain is always unjust – and arguments
that cannot flatter increase suspicion.
Here is Britannicus, I'll leave you now.
You can hear and pity his sad disgrace
and perhaps realise blame lies at the door
of one whose advice Nero now avoids.

SCENE THREE

Agrippina, Britannicus, Narcissus, Albine.

Agrippina

Prince, where are you running in such distress?
What brings you here to your enemy's lair?
What do you want?

13

Britannicus
  What do I want?
  Nothing more than what I've lost in this place.
  Last night a thousand uncouth soldiers came
  and dragged Junia by force to the palace.
  Imagine what her timid spirit felt?
  The horror of this unexpected call?
  She's been taken from me: a fearsome law
  will sunder two hearts united by grief.
  We'll be forbidden to mingle our pain
  in case we help one another bear it.

Agrippina
  Enough. I feel your wrongs as my own,
  I was protesting before you came here –
  but it's not with a powerless anger
  that I'll fulfil the promises I made.
  I won't go further: if you want to hear more,
  come to Pallas's house. I'll expect you.

SCENE FOUR

Britannicus, Narcissus.

Britannicus
  Can I trust her, Narcissus? Will she
  take sides with me against her own son?
  Isn't she still the same Agrippina
  whom my father married for his ruin
  and who, you say, when his last days dragged on,
  ended them herself to pursue her plans?

Narcissus
  So? She feels as indignant as you do.
  She had promised you Junia in marriage.
  Unite your grief, entwine your ambitions.
  This palace always echoes with your cries:

but as long as you're only complaining
and people feel pity rather than fear,
as long as mere words contain your anger,
your lot will be to complain for ever.

Britannicus

Narcissus, you know that I don't intend
to accept this enslavement for ever.
You see whether I agree to renounce
this empire I was not meant to lose –
but I am still alone. My father's friends
are all strangers, cooled by my misfortune,
and my very youth keeps all those away
who in their hearts might still want me to rule.
It's only a year since I've understood
the sad fate that's been allotted to me –
and what do I find but friends who've been bought,
who follow me only to spy on me,
who, chosen by Nero, for this foul task
transact with him the secrets of my soul?
Narcissus, I am duped and sold every day –
he knows my plans, hears everything I say,
he knows as well as you what's in my heart –
is that not so?

Narcissus

Who would be so shameless?
You should only speak to those you can trust –
Be more careful when you express your thoughts.

Britannicus

You speak well, Narcissus, but suspicion
does not dwell in an honourable heart.
One remains dupe too long – but I accept
and vow from now on to trust only you.
My father, I remember, praised your zeal –
you're the only freed slave who's remained true.
Your eyes, always watching my behaviour

have saved me from many a hidden trap.
Go now, discover if this new outrage
has inspired courage in my allies.
Observe their looks, listen to what they say.
Unearth any who will come to my aid.
And especially here, in this palace, watch
how Nero treats the princess, how she's kept –
find out if she's recovered from her fears
and if I will be allowed to see her.
I will go now and seek Agrippina
at the house of Pallas – like you, a freed slave.
I'll see her, provoke her and use her name
to take things further than she ever planned.

End of Act One.

Act Two

Nero, Burrhus, Narcissus.

Nero

She's my mother, Burrhus, I can forgive
her injustices, all her caprices
but I refuse to forgive or ignore
that insolent minister who rules her.
Pallas is a poisonous adviser –
he's now trying to seduce my brother.
Enough. I'll keep him away from them both.
I want Pallas to go now. Far away.
I want it. I order it. Let this day
not come to end with Pallas in Rome.
Go. This edict is for Rome's own welfare.
You, Narcissus, come here. And you, leave us.

SCENE TWO

Nero, Narcissus.

Narcissus

Thank the gods, my lord, Junia in your hands
will bring all wavering Romans to your side.
The hopes of your enemies are shattered –
they've gone to Pallas to mourn their lost power.
But what do I see? You look shocked, dismayed,
you seem even more stunned than your brother.
What does this strange and sudden sadness mean?
These dark looks darting hither and thither?
Fortune smiles on you, she obeys your will.

Nero
Narcissus. It's done. Nero is in love.

Narcissus
You?

Nero
Just now but for the rest of my life.
I love – do I say love? I worship her.

Narcissus
You love Junia –

Nero
It was curiosity –
I saw her come to the palace last night.
She lifted her tear-filled eyes to the skies,
tears that glinted more brightly than weapons, flames –
Lovely, without ornaments, and simply
dressed with the beauty of one still asleep.
What can I say? Was it this scant cover,
the shadows, torches, cries and then silence
or the fierce look of those who were holding her
bringing out the soft shyness of her eyes?
I don't know – I was entranced by this sight –
I tried to speak to her, my voice left me.
I was rooted to the spot, struck, amazed,
and I let her walk by me to her rooms.
I went to my own rooms and there, alone,
I tried to free myself from her image.
But she was there, before my eyes, I spoke
to her – my love ignited by her tears –
those tears I had caused. Sometimes – but too late –
I asked for her forgiveness, using sighs
or, when I needed to, terrible threats.
That's how I spent the whole night – without sleep:
but perhaps I've embellished her image –
she appeared to me in too soft a light.
What do you think, Narcissus?

Narcissus
Ask rather –
how could she have escaped you for so long?

Nero
Whether she was angry for her brother
and blamed me for driving him to his death,
or whether her heart, proud, sober and fierce
has a beauty she didn't wish us to see,
she's remained faithful to her suffering,
locked away in shade and hiding from fame.
And it's this virtue, this tenacity,
so new in this court that has excited me.
Think, Narcissus, there is no girl in Rome
whom my love does not flatter and make vain.
As soon as I have set eyes on a face,
she runs here to try out Nero's heart.
Alone in her palace, the modest Junia
takes Nero's attentions as an insult,
escapes and does not try to discover
if Nero can be loved or is loving.
Tell me this: does Britannicus love her?

Narcissus
Are you asking if he loves her, my lord?

Nero
He's so young, does he know himself so well?
Has he already tasted love's poison?

Narcissus
My lord, love does not wait on our reason.
Don't doubt it, he loves her, he sees her charms.
He has experience of her tears and knows
how to accommodate all her wishes.
And maybe he knows how to persuade her.

Nero
You mean he may hold sway over her heart?

Narcissus

Who knows, my lord, but I can say this much:
I've seen Britannicus leave the palace
brimming with an anger he hid from you –
complaining of the court's ingratitude,
tired of your grandeur, his insignificance,
floating between his fear and his ambition –
he would see Junia and come back smiling.

Nero

Let him wish rather for Junia's anger:
no one makes me jealous and goes unscathed.

Narcissus

My lord, what can possibly worry you?
Junia might have shared and pitied his pain:
she would have seen no other tears but his –
but today, my lord, her eyes will open
as she sees the brilliance that emanates
from you, who make kings vanish in the crowd.
She'll see her beloved lost among them,
glued to your eyes, trembling with the honour
of one glance you might have bestowed by chance.
When she sees how, from this glorious height, you
offer her with your sighs a conquered heart,
don't doubt it, my lord, her heart will succumb:
demand to be loved and you will be loved.

Nero

I fear I'll be thwarted at every turn –
interference –

Narcissus

What stops you, my lord?

Nero

Everything: Octavia, Agrippina,
Burrhus, Seneca and then all of Rome –
three years of virtue – not that Octavia

holds back my heart or that I feel sorry.
I'm tired of looking at her – her tears
only make me want to run out faster.
I'll be only too happy if divorce
frees me from this yoke I was forced to bear.
Even the heavens seem to condemn her.
She's unable to produce Nero's heir
which the empire keeps demanding in vain.
For four years now all her hopes have been dashed.

Narcissus

Repudiate her now, why wait so long?
The empire and your heart condemn her.
How long will you go against your desires –
or do you not dare seek your own pleasures?

Nero

Is there not my implacable mother?
I can see her now drag Octavia here
and with a raging look remind her son
that she tied this knot – and she'll compound it
with a long list of my ingratitudes.
How am I to face these unwelcome rants?

Narcissus

Are you not, my lord, her master and yours?
Will you tremble before her for ever?
You rule for yourself, why rule for her sake?

Nero

I can order, threaten, away from her.
I listen to your advice, I agree.
I rouse myself against her, ready
to confront her – until she looks at me.
And – to lay my naked soul before you –
I can't seem to challenge the great power
of those eyes where I still read my duty.
Perhaps I'm faithful to the memory

of all I owe for what she did for me.
However I try – it comes to nothing.
My will is stunned and paralysed by hers.
I try to free myself from this slavery,
I run away from her, I'm rude to her –
I try to provoke her irritation
so that she'll avoid me and set me free.
But I've kept you too long. Leave me alone,
Britannicus might suspect your motives.

Narcissus

No: Britannicus trusts me completely.
He thinks it's because of him I'm here now –
he wants me to discover your secrets.
Mostly he is hoping to see his love
and he thinks I'll persuade you to do so.

Nero

I will allow it – you can tell him that:
he will see her.

Narcissus

My lord, send him away –

Nero

I have my reasons. I can assure you
he'll pay dearly for the pleasures I grant –
but meantime boast of your happy stratagem.
Tell him I'm being duped by you,
that he sees her without my permission.
Here she comes, go, lead Britannicus here.

SCENE THREE

Nero, Junia.

Nero
You seem perturbed, your expression changes:
you read something in my eyes, you're frightened?

Junia
My lord, I cannot disguise my error:
I was seeking Octavia, not Nero.

Nero
I'm aware of that, I was envious
of so much kindness intended for her.

Junia
You, lord?

Nero
Is Octavia the only one
who deserves the pleasure of seeing you?

Junia
Who else could possibly show me mercy?
Who else might tell me what crime I've committed?
But since you're punishing me you must know:
I beg you, my lord, to explain my guilt.

Nero
Isn't it a crime to have remained hidden,
to have escaped my notice for so long
and to have kept yourself away from me?
When the heavens showered you with beauty
was it right to ensure it was buried?
Shouldn't the happy Britannicus beware
that his love and your charms grow far from me?
Why deny me the gift of your presence
and without a thought abandon me here?

There's more: I'm told you hear Britannicus
without demur. I hope he speaks clearly,
for I must believe the austere Junia
would promise nothing without asking me –
and that I wouldn't be told by mere rumours
that she had agreed to love and be loved.

Junia

I cannot deny, my lord, that his sighs
have occasionally betrayed his hopes.
He was not above looking at a girl
who is her shattered family's last remains.
He may remember a happier time
when his father destined me as his wife.
When he loves me, he obeys the Emperor
his father and, dare I say, your mother
as well as you – since you and she agree . . .

Nero

My mother has her plans and I have mine.
Let's leave out Claudius and Agrippina –
it is not for me to follow their choice.
I am the only one to speak for you
and I wish to choose your husband myself.

Junia

Lord, I come from a long line of emperors:
any other alliance would shame them.

Nero

No, the husband I have in mind for you
has a lineage as glorious as your own:
you'll feel no shame when you accept his love.

Junia

Who could this husband be, my lord?

Nero
Myself.

Junia
You?

Nero
I would suggest another
if I could find someone better than Nero.
I wanted to offer you a good choice:
I looked at the empire, the court, Rome.
I looked everywhere and the more I looked
for someone worthy of such a great treasure
the more I realised that only one man
could hold this bounty: the Emperor himself –
since everyone in Rome is in his care.
Remember your own youth, how Claudius then
had promised the empire to his son
Britannicus, with you as his consort.
The gods chose elsewhere, so you must obey
their will and the will of the empire.
As for me, I wouldn't have accepted Rome
if it did not come as well with your heart –
if such burdens could not be soothed by you –
if, when I'm beset by cares and worries
in a life plagued by envy or pity,
I could not find solace in your presence.
Don't let thoughts of Octavia concern you:
Rome as well I are in agreement
that I must divorce Octavia and cut
a marriage bond the heavens have not blessed.
Consider all this and weigh the benefits
of this choice worthy of a prince's love,
worthy of beautiful eyes kept hidden,
worthy of a universe that needs you.

Junia
My lord, it's hard not to be astounded
when on the same day I'm brought here by force
like the most common criminal of Rome,

then suddenly offered Octavia's place.
Allow me to say I have neither deserved
this excess of honour nor of debasement.
How could you want, my lord, to make a girl
who saw as she was born her family ruined,
who nourished her pain in obscurity
and found virtue in accepting misery,
move suddenly from this quiet retreat
to a rank exposing her to the world –
when I did everything to hide from it –
and where another holds her rightful place?

Nero

I told you, I'm divorcing Octavia.
Have less fear or at least less modesty.
Don't think my choice is not well considered.
I can answer for you: only agree.
Remember your family's nobility.
I offer you honour, don't choose instead
the glory of a 'no' you might regret.

Junia

My Lord, the Heavens know my deepest thoughts:
a mad glory does not appeal to me.
I see the immensity of your gift
but the greater the spendour of this rank
the more I would feel shame as I perceived
I had snatched it from its rightful owner.

Nero

You seem much too concerned for Octavia.
These marks of friendship are rather excessive.
But let's be direct and speak clearly now:
the sister matters less than the brother?
Britannicus –

Junia

– has touched my heart, my lord.
I will not pretend it is otherwise.

Perhaps this truthfulness lacks discretion
but I always speak what is in my heart.
I'm not at court, I didn't learn to practise
the art of saying what I do not think.
I love Britannicus. I was promised
to him when the empire would follow.
But the misery that kept him from the throne –
his honour taken away, his palace
deserted by the court and left empty –
are so many bonds that tie him to me.
When Nero wants something, he gets it.
Your untroubled days are spent in pleasure
which Rome's empire is glad to provide.
And if anything comes to disturb you
the whole world tries to make you feel better.
Britannicus must suffer by himself:
I am the only one who cares for him.
His only joy, my lord, are a few tears
which sometimes help him to forget his pain.

Nero

It's this joy and these tears that I envy.
Anyone else would have paid with his life –
but this prince will have a more gentle fate.
He's to come here and see you before long.

Junia

My lord! I was right to trust your virtue.

Nero

I could have forbidden his presence
but I wish to prevent the grave danger
into which his rage will no doubt lure him.
I won't destroy him. I'd rather he heard
of his fate from the one he so adores.
If you care for his life, send him away –
and don't let him suspect my jealousy.
Be the one who demands his banishment.

You can use words or you can use silence –
let your cold manner make him understand
his hopes and desires must lie elsewhere.

Junia
How could I condemn him to this despair?
I have sworn differently a thousand times.
Even if my words could betray me now
he'll know from my eyes not to believe me.

Nero
I'll be hidden nearby, I will watch you.
Place your love in your heart's deepest dungeon.
You will have no language secret from me,
I'll hear looks that you believe are silent
and any gesture or sigh that escapes
and offers him hope – will cost him his life.

Junia
My lord, if I dare ask for one thing more
don't let me see Britannicus again.

SCENE FOUR

Nero, Junia, Narcissus.

Narcissus
Britannicus asks to see the princess –
He's coming –

Nero
Let him come.

Junia
My lord –

Nero
He's here –
Remember: he's in your hands now – not mine.
And when you look at him, I look at you.

28

Junia, Narcissus.

Junia

Run to him, Narcissus, quickly – warn him –
but he's already here – and now we're lost.

SCENE SIX

Junia, Britannicus, Narcissus.

Britannicus

Oh the bliss of being near you once more!
But in the midst of delight, what torment!
Will I be able to see you again?
Must I go through a thousand contortions
for the joy I once savoured every day?
What a night – brute awakening – were you
able to disarm your gaolers' insolence?
Where was your lover? What malevolent
spirit kept me from dying for your sake?
In the middle of your terrors did you
call to me in secret that I might help?
Did you wish for my presence, dear princess?
Did you know what torment I would suffer?
You're silent? Is this your greeting? This ice?
That's not a look to soothe my injuries.
Speak. We're alone. I've tricked our enemies.
I know they're busy elsewhere – we can talk.
Quick! let's take advantage of their absence –

Junia

This palace you're in exudes his power.
These very walls could be looking at us.
The Emperor is never far from here.

Britannicus
And since when are you so afraid of him?
Why do you feel you should hide your feelings?
What happened to the heart that swore a love
that you claimed even Nero would envy?
Listen, believe me, there's nothing to fear.
People's hearts have not turned against us:
all of Rome disapproves of Nero's act.
Nero's mother, Agrippina, is ours –

Junia
My lord, you speak against your real thoughts.
How many times didn't you yourself tell me
that all Rome was singing Nero's praises?
You could always recognise his virtue.
You speak like that now because you're in pain.

Britannicus
I'm rather surprised by the way you speak –
I didn't come to you to hear Nero praised.
I manage to find a little moment
to share with you a pain that overwhelms
and you can only use this precious time
to praise the enemy who destroys me?
What's made you so unlike yourself today?
Even your look is without expression.
What do I see? Eyes that refuse to meet mine.
Does Nero attract you? Am I repulsed?
If I believed that, oh – by the heavens –
don't torment my soul any more, please, speak –
don't you remember what I've been to you?

Junia
Leave me, please, the Emperor is coming.

She goes.

Britannicus
After this, Narcissus, whom can I trust?

SCENE SEVEN

Nero, Junia, Narcissus.

Nero
And so . . .

Junia
No, I won't listen to more now –
you've been obeyed – let me at least shed tears
without having you inspect those as well.

SCENE EIGHT

Nero, Narcissus.

Nero
Did you see all that? Even her silence
couldn't mask the raging fire of their love.
I can't be deceived, she loves my brother:
I'll have to console myself with his pain.
I had a lovely image of despair
when I saw him doubt his beloved's heart.
I'll follow her. My rival waits for you
to unburden himself. Go, run, tease him,
encourage his suspicions, torment him.
If I must witness how he's loved and mourned
let him not know it and pay for it dear.

He leaves.

Narcissus (*alone*)
For a second time Fortune beckons you,
Narcissus, how could you resist its voice?
Let us follow its commands to the end
and build our good luck on their destruction.

End of Act Two.

Act Three

Nero, Burrhus.

Burrhus
Pallas will obey, my lord.

Nero
And how does
my mother take Pallas's punishment?

Burrhus
There's no doubt she feels the blow badly.
She won't accept it without reproaches.
She's been shouting her outrage for some time.
We must hope she will do no more than shout.

Nero
What plots could she possibly be hatching?

Burrhus
Agrippina is always a danger.
Her family is worshipped by all of Rome –
your soldiers still remember her father.
She knows her power, you know her courage.
And what is concerning me even more
is that her anger now looks justified –
you provide her with the weapons she needs.

Nero
Me, Burrhus?

Burrhus
My lord, this new love of yours –

Nero
I've heard you, Burrhus, but there is no cure –

32

my heart has spoken stronger words than yours –
Nero must love –

Burrhus

That's what you believe now.
You're convinced you can't banish this evil
because you've encountered some resistance,
but if your heart held firm to its duty –
refused to listen to this enemy –
if you hold fast to your past behaviour
and if you deign to think of Octavia
whose virtues don't deserve this banishment –
and then if you can avoid setting eyes
on Junia for a few days, you will see
that however strong this love seems to you
no one has to love when they don't want to.

Nero

Burrhus, when a warning calls us to war
or, sitting in the senate in peace time,
I have to decide on the fate of Rome,
then I'll listen to you, take your advice.
But love is a very different science
which ill suits your austerity. No need
for you to stoop to find a remedy:
I'm in too much pain when I'm far from her.

He leaves.

SCENE TWO

Burrhus alone.

Burrhus

Well, now Nero reveals his true nature.
This ferocity I thought I could curb
wants to break free from my feeble constraints.

33

How far will it go, to what excesses?
What can I do? Who will help me act now?
Seneca could help me, but he's away.
What about Agrippina? If I could
rekindle her love for him then I might . . .
but she's coming – here's my chance with her now –

SCENE THREE

Agrippina, Burrhus, Albine.

Agrippina
Your lessons seem to have had great success.
Pallas is exiled, when his only crime
was to have brought your master to the throne.
You know that without his advice Claudius
would not have adopted my son.
And now Nero's wife has a new rival
and my son breaks free from his marriage vows.
What good work from one who hates flattery –
the ministerial aide whose duty was
to curb my son's youthful ardour –
you nourish it and encourage him to
despise his mother and forget his wife.

Burrhus
You're so quick to accuse me, my lady.
Until now Nero has done nothing wrong:
Pallas was courting exile with his pride
and his downfall was unavoidable.
The Emperor only did with regret
what all of Rome demanded in secret.
As for the rest, the harm can be undone.
We can stem the course of Octavia's tears.
But please stop all your recriminations.
You can bring him back to his wife gently.
Threats, cries, and harsh words only make him flee.

Agrippina

So now you want to try to curb my tongue:
you think I'm afraid of my own creature.
Pallas may be exiled but I still have
the support I need to avenge my fall.
Britannicus has begun to resent
my crimes against him, which I now regret.
You know I can show him to the army
and rouse their pity at his oppression.
And then I'll ask them to give him justice.
On one side they will see Claudius's son,
who'll urge them to remember his father,
reminding them of their old allegiance –
and me – the daughter of Germanicus.
On the other side, Enobarbus's son,
Nero, flanked by Seneca and Burrhus,
whom I myself called back from exile –
but who now want to become the masters.
I will tell them what crimes we committed
and they can learn how Nero came to rule.
I'll acknowledge the bloodiest rumours
to make his power and yours more hateful.
I'll withhold nothing: exile and murders,
even poison –

Burrhus

– and they won't believe you.
They'll recognise your strategic attempt
to harm Nero by self-accusation.
As for me, who approved all of your plans
and made the army swear its allegiance,
I still don't repent of my zeal for him.
He's the son and the heir to Claudius:
Claudius gave him that right by adoption
and replaced Britannicus with Nero
so Rome would chose him as her emperor.
Tiberius, adopted by Augustus, was also chosen

35

and the young Agrippa, the rightful heir,
had to forego his claim to the empire.
With such precedents you cannot weaken
Nero's legitimate claim to power.
And if he still listens to me, I hope
that Nero's kindness will make you desist.
I've begun – I plan to continue my work.

SCENE FOUR

Agrippina, Albine.

Albine
Your suffering rages uncontrollably,
my lady, what if Nero could hear you –?

Agrippina
Then let me see Nero with my own eyes!

Albine
Why show such concern for Britannicus?
Or Junia? why sacrifice your own peace?
Why control Nero even in his loves?

Agrippina
Can't you see to what I'll now be reduced?
I'm being presented with a rival!
If I don't break this unfortunate bond,
my place will be taken, I'll be nothing.
Until now, Octavia had no power –
empress only in name, ignored by all.
I held in my hands all grace, all favour –
and everyone came to me with their needs –
But the one who can capture Nero's heart
will have the power of wife and mistress.
All the care and the glory of the court
will be hers – one look from her will decide –

Already I'm neglected, left alone . . .
No, I can't bear even to think of it –
ungrateful Nero – but here's his rival.

SCENE FIVE

Britannicus, Agrippina, Narcissus, Albine.

Britannicus
Our enemies are not invincible.
Our treatment has moved some hearts to pity.
While we were wasting our time lamenting,
our friends – until now so discreet – were fuelled
by this injustice and found Narcissus.
Nero cannot discard my sister and
enjoy this woman with impunity.
If you are still concerned for Octavia,
we can force Nero to honour his vows.
Half of the senate believes in our cause:
There's Plautus, Scylla, Piso –

Agrippina
Is it so?
Plautus, Scylla, Piso – are powerful . . .

Britannicus
I see you would prefer it were not so,
that your anger, shaken, irresolute,
is frightened of obtaining what it seeks.
Don't worry, you sealed my disgrace so well
that no friend will show courage for my sake.

Agrippina
Britannicus, don't be so suspicious.
We can only be saved if we're allies –
I promised, that's enough. Your enemies
cannot make me break a promise I made.

37

Nero can try to avoid my anger:
sooner or later he'll hear his mother.
I will then try to persuade or threaten,
and if I fail I'll bring forth your sister –
and who wouldn't be won over by her tears?
Then Rome will feel her grief and my power.
I'll besiege Nero relentlessly but –
you must try to avoid being seen by him.

SCENE SIX

Britannicus, Narcissus.

Britannicus
> Have you tried to console me with false hopes?
> Can I really believe what you have said,
> Narcissus?

Narcissus
> You can indeed, my lord, but
> this is not the place to unveil such things.
> Let's go. What are you waiting for?

Britannicus
> Waiting? Narcissus –

Narcissus
> There is nothing here.

Britannicus
> Could you not find a way, some stratagem –?

Narcissus
> For what?

Britannicus
> Narcissus: for me to see her.
> It makes me blush but I still want to hear
> what she has to say now she is more calm.

Narcissus
After all I've told you, you still trust her?

Britannicus
No, I think Junia faithless, cruel, worthy
of all my rage against her, but I feel
that despite myself I can't believe this.
My heart is confused but also stubborn.
I find excuses – I still worship her.
I want to hate her with tranquillity.
How can I believe that a heart that seemed
so noble and hated all pomp
would betray itself, display in one day
a cold treachery unknown even here?

Narcissus
How do we know she didn't plan long ago
to entangle Nero and vanquish him?
She was elusive so she could ensnare.
She ran away the better to be caught
and excite in Nero the desire
to break a pride that seemed unbendable.

Britannicus
Then I mustn't see her?

Narcissus
No, at this time
a new lover is fawning at her feet.

Britannicus
Very well, let's go, but look, here she is –

Narcissus (*leaving*)
I have to warn the Emperor about this!

Britannicus, Junia.

Junia
Britannicus, run, escape from this place
where my love for you excites such anger.
Nero's furious, his mother's ambushed him –
and I managed to escape to come here.
Go, keep yourself safe, don't break my heart
and one day you'll know the depth of my love.
Your image is engraved deep in my soul –
nothing can erase it.

Britannicus
I hear you well –
You want my absence to seal your triumph
and clear the path for your more recent love.
It must be that when you see me, some shame
creeps into your pleasures and disturbs them.
Very well, I'll leave –

Junia
If only I could . . .

Britannicus
If only you could have resisted more.
I'm not surprised that an ordinary heart
should be attracted by wealth, by power,
that Rome's empire might dazzle your eyes
and that you'd like to take my sister's place,
but you seemed so immune to temptation –
indifferent to the empire's glitter.
And I admit my heart was duped too long:
I cannot get used to this misery.
I saw the heavens ruin me unjustly –
they rewarded all of my enemies.

But this wasn't cruel enough punishment:
there remained to be forgotten by you.

Junia

I would make you take back all of those words –
if times were better – but Nero threatens,
and you're in danger – I want to save you.
Go, stop these reproaches, Nero was there,
listening. I had no choice but to pretend.

Britannicus

What, his cruelty –

Junia

– made him watch my face –
spying on every expression of mine.
His revenge would have been swift and brutal
If he'd seen us agreeing together.

Britannicus

If Nero was listening why couldn't your eyes
show more kindness and offer me a sign?
Is love mute? Has it only one language?
One look would have preserved me from torment.
You could –

Junia

– only keep quiet and save you.
How many times – I'll tell you everything –
I wanted to show you my turmoil.
How many sighs did I have to hold back,
avoid the eyes I was always seeking.
What a torment to watch the one I love
suffer so – and to keep punishing him.
I didn't feel I could pretend well enough –
I kept fearing that an angry Nero
would insist I still wanted to please you.
I was afraid my love would break its chains –
and I wished then that I had never loved –

but alas Nero knows only too well
that we love each other. Go now and hide
I have many more secrets to reveal –

Britannicus

Oh – this is too much, my doubts, your goodness,
and all you're sacrificing for my sake –
I'm sorry – forgive me – here – at your feet –

Junia

What are you doing? Nero is coming!

SCENE EIGHT

Nero, Britannicus, Junia.

Nero

Don't mind me, prince, or stop this touching show.
I judge her kindness by your gratitude.
So I find him at your feet, my lady.
Then he'll also have good cause to thank me:
this place brings him such luck I'll keep you here –
and facilitate your future meetings –

Britannicus

I can lay my joy or pain at her feet,
wherever she will consent to see me
and this place where you keep her imprisoned
does not fill me with dread when I see it.

Nero

Have you not seen anything that tells you
that I deserve respect and obedience?

Britannicus

These walls did not see us both being raised
for you to give orders or me to obey.
They did not foresee when they saw us born
that I'd be ruled by my father's stepson.

Nero
Since then our destinies have crossed over:
I obeyed you then, you obey me now.
You may not have learned yet how to submit –
but you're still very young: you can be taught.

Britannicus
Who is there to teach me?

Nero
The empire.

Britannicus
When did Rome bestow on you the right
to injustice, cruelty and kidnap
as well as imprisonment, rape, divorce?

Nero
Rome does not delve into private matters
and respects what I do not wish to show.
Do the same.

Britannicus
We know what Rome is thinking.

Nero
Rome keeps quiet, imitate her silence.

Britannicus
Has Nero begun to lose self-control?

Nero
Nero's begun to tire of your words.

Britannicus
Rome was so happy to have Nero reign.

Nero
Happy or not, it's enough that I'm feared.

Britannicus
If I know Junia, such an admission
will never meet with her heart's approval.

Nero

It may not be easy to please Junia
but punishing her lover is child's play.

Britannicus

For me the only threat I really fear
is the thought of displeasing the one I love.

Nero

If I were you, I would pray for that now.

Britannicus

My only ambition is to please her.

Nero

You'll always please her: she's promised as much.

Britannicus

At least I don't stoop to eavesdrop on her
and she can say what she feels about me:
I don't have to spy to keep her silent.

Nero

I understand you. Very well. Soldiers!

Junia

What are you doing? You are both brothers.
My lord, these are the words of a jealous lover.
He is beset by a thousand troubles.
How can you envy his morsel of joy?
I'll disappear, keep away from you both
and so remove the cause of your hatred.
You need no longer resent my promises:
only the gods will have them from now on.
My lord, I will join the vestal virgins.

Nero

Dear lady, this is too unexpected.
Soldiers, take her back to her apartment
and keep Britannicus with his sister.

Britannicus

This is how Nero woos the one he loves.

Junia

Britannicus, let's not oppose his will.

Nero

Soldiers, stop delaying and obey me!

SCENE NINE

Burrhus, Nero.

Burrhus

What do I see? Heavens, what is all this?

Nero

And so their love only burns more brightly.
I know the hand that brought them together.
Agrippina only stopped me just now
and made me listen to her endless speech
so that she could give them time together.
Go – find my mother and if she's still here,
Burrhus, I want her kept in this palace,
and her own guards to be replaced by mine.

Burrhus

My lord, without hearing her? A mother?

Nero

Burrhus I don't know what plots you're hatching
but for some days now anything I ask
finds in you an irritating censor.
Take care of her and if you choose not to
I'll find others who'll take care of you both.

End of Act Three.

Act Four

Agrippina, Burrhus.

Burrhus
Yes, you can put forward your defence now.
Nero himself is coming to hear you.
If he had you restrained in this palace
it was perhaps only to speak with you.
Whatever the reason, may I suggest
that you forget he has offended you.
Defend yourself, yes, but don't accuse him.
He is the only one Rome considers.
He may be your son and your creation
but he's also your emperor and, like us,
you must obey that power you gave him.
The way he acts towards you – with threats or love –
will make people seek you or keep away.
When people come to you it's for his sake,
remember that. Here he is –

Agrippina
You can leave us.

SCENE TWO

Agrippina, Nero. Agrippina sits.

Agrippina
Come here, Nero, and sit by your mother.
I've been told I need to assuage your doubts
but I don't know of what crimes I'm accused.
Let me lay before you all of my deeds.

46

You rule and you know how far from your grasp
the empire stood the day you were born.
The list of my ancestors who ruled Rome
could not help you become its new emperor.
There was only one way: when Claudius's wife,
the mother of Britannicus, was killed
a thousand beauties tried to take her place.
I sought the bed of Claudius with one plan:
to give you the throne where I would be placed.
I bent my pride, I sought Pallas's help,
Claudius was my uncle, I seduced him –
but he didn't dare break the laws of incest.
The senate was bribed, the laws changed and I had
Claudius in my bed and Rome at my feet.
It was a lot for me, not much for you:
thus you came into the Emperor's orbit.
You became his stepson, then son-in-law
when I gave you his daughter as your wife.
Silenus who loved her, his hopes thwarted,
killed himself on the day you were married.
But that wasn't enough: there was still one
more obstacle: Britannicus himself –
the legitimate son of the Emperor.
How to make Claudius prefer his stepson?
I sought once again the aid of Pallas:
he persuaded Claudius to adopt you.
Claudius named you Nero and decided
to introduce you early to power.
It was then that people began to see
my plans, which were by then too well advanced.
They saw Britannicus's future doom
and began to whisper to his father.
My lavish promises stopped some of them –
the worst were quickly sent into exile.
Claudius himself was by now exhausted.
I sent away from him all those whose zeal

47

could have saved the throne for Britannicus.
I did more: I chose from base followers
those who would look after his upbringing.
For you, I did the very opposite
and found you tutors respected by Rome,
men whose reputation was the highest.
I did not choose them for my sake but yours.
I called back from exile and the army
that very same Seneca, that Burrhus,
who now – but Rome believed in their virtue.
Then I emptied the coffers of Claudius
to distribute largesses in your name:
spectacles, games, presents, all drew to you
the hearts of the people and the army,
soldiers who in any case remembered
your grandfather, the great Germanicus.
But when Claudius was nearing his end he
suddenly saw what he had been blind to
and tried too late to call his friends for help.
I controlled his guards, his palace, his bed –
I made sure his renewed love for his son
remained fruitless, I monitored his sighs –
I looked after him as if to spare him
more pain – but as he lay dying, I hid
his son's tears from him. He died. Rumours flew.
I kept the news of his death from Rome.
Burrhus went in secret to the army
and made them swear to come over to you.
As the people prayed for Claudius's health
the Roman legions made you their ruler.
Then Claudius was brought out and the people
learned in one day he had died and you ruled.
These are my crimes and this is my reward:
you savoured the fruits of my well-laid plans
and for six months you displayed gratitude.
And then, as if ashamed of the respect

you had shown, you began to ignore me.
I watched both Burrhus and Seneca feed
your paranoia and give you lessons
in ingratitude: now you've surpassed them.
You've surrounded yourself with flatterers
whose only distinction is debauchery.
And when at last I'm wearied by your slights
and ask you why you behave so badly
you take the recourse of the ungrateful
and pile more injuries on your insults.
I've promised Junia to Britannicus:
they've believed the promise of your mother.
What happens? Junia is kidnapped at night
and suddenly becomes your lust object.
I see Octavia erased from your heart
and the bonds I tied between you broken.
Pallas is exiled, your brother is seized
and even my freedom is now curtailed.
Burrhus dares to manhandle your mother.
And when I see you at last and expect
some contrition I end up in the dock.

Nero

I don't forget I owe you the empire:
you might have relied on my gratitude
and spared yourself so much repetition.
You see, your suspicions and incessant
complaints make everyone who can hear them
believe – and I say this between ourselves –
that you have worked for yourself, not for me.
'If so many honours, such lavish gifts,
represent ingratitude on his part –'
I'm only repeating what they say –
'and if she condemns her son all the time,
are there other crimes that he's committed?
Did she crown Nero to make him obey?
Is he then the guardian of her power?'

49

And yet, if I could have satisfied you
I would have offered you that power which
your incessant laments seem to demand –
but Rome wants a master, not a mistress.
Every day the senate and the people,
tired of hearing your orders through me,
start whispering that Claudius, when he died,
left me his throne but also his weakness.
Anyone else would have listened to this
but you grumble unless you rule supreme.
And now you join forces with my brother
and plot with the supporters of Junia.
I can see Pallas's hands in these plots.
I put a stop to them but your anger
now wants to sway the army against me
and – I'm told – offer them Britannicus.

Agrippina
Why would I make Britannicus emperor?
How could you believe that? Why would I act
in this way? What would I expect from it?
What honours would his reign bring me, what rank?
If under your rule I am never spared,
if they always condemn Nero's mother,
what would happen to me under his rule?
I would be accused not of complaining
but of real crimes I committed for you
and for which I would be quickly condemned.
But you don't deceive me, I see your plan.
You have no gratitude, you never did:
from your early years all my care, my love
and tenderness were met with indifference.
Nothing softened you – and your callousness
should have put an end to my bounty.
How unhappy I am, what misfortune
to find all that I've done dismissed by you!
I have only one son, O you heavens,

did I ever invoke you but for him?
Wasn't everything I prayed for – for him?
Remorse, fear, dangers, nothing stopped me.
I ignored his scorn, dire predictions
of how he would treat me in the future.
I did what I could: you rule, that's enough.
And since you've taken away my freedom
you can now take my life if you want to –
as long as the people don't turn and take back
all that it cost me so much to give you.

Nero
Fine. Tell me then. What do you want from me?

Agrippina
Let those who dared accuse me be punished
and the anger of Britannicus soothed.
Let Junia choose the husband she wishes.
Let them both be free and Pallas recalled.
Let me see you any time I want to
and let that Burrhus now listening outside
stop guarding your door against your mother.

Nero
I want my immense gratitude towards you
to etch your power on everyone's heart.
I'm pleased we had this little argument:
it will reignite our great affection.
Let's forget whatever Pallas has done.
Let me embrace Britannicus again.
You will now be the final arbiter
over that love that tore us asunder.
Go then, bring the good news to my brother.
Guards, take all your orders from my mother.

SCENE THREE

Nero, Burrhus.

Burrhus
How this peace and these embraces touch me!
And you know that's all I ever wanted
and that I never opposed your friendship
or deserved her unjustified wrath.

Nero
I won't deceive you, I suspected you –
I thought the two of you in agreement.
Her antagonism makes me trust you.
But she's in too great a hurry to win:
I embrace my rival to smother him.

Burrhus
What, my lord?

Nero
I've had enough. His ruin now
will deliver me from my mother's threats.
She keeps casting his shadow over me:
I'm only half alive while he still breathes.
I'm not about to let her scheming promise
my brother my place for a second time.

Burrhus
And so she will soon mourn Britannicus?

Nero
When this day ends I'll no longer fear him.

Burrhus
And who has inspired such a desire?

Nero
My glory, love, well-being and my life.

Burrhus
   Whatever you say, it's impossible
   that you would conceive of such a vile act.

Nero
   Burrhus!

Burrhus
   How can I hear this from your mouth?
   How could you hear of this and not tremble?
   Do you know with what blood you'll soon be drenched?
   Is Nero tired of ruling all hearts?

Nero
   So: I have to remain chained to past glories
   and keep in front of me this so-called love
   which chance gives us one day then takes away.
   Did I become emperor to please others,
   submit to their wishes and foil my own?

Burrhus
   What better wishes could you have, my lord,
   than to bring happiness to your subjects?
   It's for you to choose: you're still the master.
   You've been a good man, you can stay that way.
   You can proceed from virtue to virtue,
   but if you follow some of your courtiers
   you will have to descend from crime to crime,
   affirm your actions by greater cruelty
   as you wash with blood the blood from your hands.
   Your brother won't die without arousing
   the zeal of friends who'll want to avenge him.
   And those friends will be followed by others
   who when they too die will have followers.
   The fires you start will never go out.
   You'll be feared but yourself always afraid,
   able only to punish or tremble
   and see all of your subjects as enemies.
   How can these first years of a happy reign

make you hate, my lord, your own innocence?
Is there no pleasure in thinking – saying –
'I'm loved and revered wherever I go.
There is no alarm when they hear my name.
People's hearts are lifted when I walk by.'
These were your pleasures. Heavens! What a change.
You valued the lowest of your subjects.
I remember the day when the senate
had condemned a man to death and asked
you to sign the decree. You resisted.
You accused your own heart of cruelty.
'I wish,' you said, 'I didn't know how to write –'
No, please listen to me or let me die,
I do not wish to live if I must watch
Nero commit such a horrible act.

On his knees.

I'm ready, my lord, and before you go,
put your sword through this heart that won't consent.
Call those who could inspire such cruelty,
let them practise their dark deed first with me.
But I think my tears have touched my emperor.
Your virtue shudders before their frenzy.
Waste no more time and give me the names
of those traitors who dare advise this bloodbath.
Call your brother – in his embrace forget –

Nero
Ah, what are you asking?

Burrhus
He doesn't hate you –
He is betrayed himself, he is guileless.
I'll answer for him, for his obedience.
I'll make sure you can speak to each other.

Nero
Let him wait with you in my apartments.

SCENE FOUR

Narcissus, Nero.

Narcissus
    I've arranged everything for this just death.
    The poison's ready, sharper than the sword.

Nero
    Narcissus, enough, I'm grateful to you
    but don't want you to go any further.

Narcissus
    Why? Has your hatred of Britannicus weakened?
    You forbid –

Nero
    It's been arranged, we're now friends.

Narcissus
    It's not for me to stop this course of yours –
    but – my lord – he's just found himself in prison.
    He won't forget this very easily.
    And time eventually reveals all things.
    He'll know he was meant to receive from me
    the poison that you had ordered for him.
    I hope the heavens distract him from this
    but he might act with the boldness you lack.

Nero
    His heart is guaranteed, I'll control mine.

Narcissus
    And you'll seal this with Junia's marriage vows?
    You'll also sacrifice your love for her?

Nero
    This is not your concern. In any case,
    I don't consider him my enemy.

Narcissus

    Agrippina was right and she can boast
    that she's got back her power over you.

Nero

    What's this? What did she say? What do you mean?

Narcissus

    She was crowing publicly about you.

Nero

    Saying what?

Narcissus

    Oh, that all she had to do
    was give you one look and you'd be frozen
    into abject silence, all anger spent,
    and that you'd be the first to sue for peace,
    only hoping that she'd deign to forgive you.

Nero

    But Narcissus, tell me, what can I do?
    I would love to punish her arrogance
    and make sure that her unabashed boasting
    was followed by the most stinging regrets.
    But how will the world speak of Nero?
    Do you want me to take the tyrant's path
    so that Rome will forget my glorious deeds
    and know me only as a poisoner?
    My vengeance will be called a fratricide.

Narcissus

    Since when are you guided by Rome's caprice?
    Have you forgotten your own desires?
    Must you believe everyone but yourself?
    It seems you don't know what Romans are like.
    To be so wary of them makes you weak:
    they'll begin to think they deserve your fear.
    They're well used to submitting to the yoke
    and they love the hand that holds them in chains.

You'll find them always burning to please you.
You're afraid they'll call you a poisoner?
Kill the brother, abandon the sister:
however innocent these two may be
Rome will soon conclude they're guilty of crimes.
You can then name as days of ill omen
the very dates they came into the world.

Nero

No, Narcissus, I can't, I can't do this.
I promised Burrhus, I had to give in.
I don't want to betray my word to him
and give him ammunition against me.
The courage I have flinches before him.
He troubles my heart when he speaks to me.

Narcissus

Burrhus doesn't always say what he thinks.
His cunning virtue serves his own interests:
he knows your act would reduce his power.
You would be free then, my lord, and you
would make your proud masters submit.
Don't you hear what they dare say out loud?
Nero, they say, was not born to rule Rome:
he can only do or say what he's told.
Burrhus rules his heart, Seneca his mind.
His main ambition, his greatest virtue,
is racing a chariot around the course
hoping for a trophy he should despise.
He's also good at preening on the stage
where Romans can come watch his antics
and while he recites and sings songs for praise
he has soldiers whose task is to coerce
the spectators to give him some applause.
Wouldn't you like this kind of discourse silenced?

Nero

Come, Narcissus, let's see what must be done.

End of Act Four.

Act Five

Britannicus, Junia.

Britannicus
    Yes, Nero – who would have thought it? – now waits
    in his rooms to embrace me – his brother.
    He's invited all the youth to the court.
    He wants to mark with a sumptuous display
    of festivities the strength of our bond.
    He will snuff out his unfortunate love
    which caused so much pain: you now rule my fate.
    And although I've been cheated of my due
    and see him clothed in my ancestral rights,
    ever since he's relinquished with such grace
    the glorious crown of your own affections,
    I find that my heart forgives him with ease
    and concedes all the rest with no regrets.
    Think: we will never be separated.
    I can look into your eyes where I see
    neither fear nor regret at refusing
    both an empire and an emperor.
    But wait – I do see a fear in your eyes.
    You listen to me but your eyes, so sad,
    look up to the distant heavens for help.
    What are you afraid of?

Junia
    That I don't know –
    but I know I'm afraid –

Britannicus
    You do love me?

58

Junia
Do I love you!

Britannicus
Nero's out of the way.

Junia
Is he sincere?

Britannicus
You doubt his motives?

Junia
Nero loved me and
swore he would destroy you –
this was not long ago: he avoids me,
he seeks you. Can such a radical change
take place so quickly in someone like Nero?

Britannicus
The work was all done by Agrippina.
She thought that my ruin might bring hers with it.
I believe in the pledges she gave me –
I believe Burrhus and even Nero –
I think that like me he doesn't hide and
either hates openly or stops hating.

Junia
Don't judge the heart of others by your own:
you two follow very different paths.
I've known Nero and his court for a day
but it's enough to see that in this place
words and the heart do not move together.
There's a pleasure in betraying one's faith.
What a foreign land for you and for me.

Britannicus
You fear him, but is Nero without fear?
He wouldn't dare, by betraying us, let rise
the anger of Rome and of the senate.

He sees well now how unjust he has been.
Even Narcissus observed his remorse.
If only he had told you, princess, how –

Junia

How do you know Narcissus is honest?
What if Narcissus is betraying you?

Britannicus

But why would my heart suspect Narcissus?

Junia

I don't know, but it's your life that's at stake.
I fear Nero, I fear some destruction
stalking me. I'm filled with forebodings.
What if this peace which you're savouring
is simply covering a new treachery?
What if Nero, hating our love for each other,
plans his vengeance under cover of night?
Is he preparing to strike as I speak?
Am I seeing you for the last time now?
Prince, beware –

Britannicus

You're crying – my dear princess!
Is your heart that full of concern for me?
And this on a day when Nero, puffed up
by power, tries to blind you with his glory.
In this same place and on this very day
you shun an empire and weep for me?
Please, please put a stop to these precious tears:
I'll come back soon and ease your forebodings –
but I'll arouse suspicion if I don't go.
I leave you with a heart brimming with love.

Junia

Prince . . .

Britannicus

They wait for me, I must go –

Junia
　At least wait until they come and call you –

Agrippina, Britannicus, Junia.

Agrippina
　Prince, why this delay? Go there at once, now –
　Nero is complaining of your absence.
　The guests hold back their pleasure and joy
　which can only burst when you two embrace.
　Don't be the one to hold up such a feast.
　Go. We, my dear, will go to Octavia.

Britannicus
　There, beautiful Junia, there in peace
　embrace my sister. She's waiting for us.
　I'll follow you there as soon as I can
　and find a way to thank you, my lady.

SCENE THREE

Agrippina, Junia.

Agrippina
　Junia, if I am not wrong I could see
　tears veil your eyes as you said goodbye.
　Can you tell me what clouds seem to threaten?
　Do you question a peace I've arranged myself?

Junia
　The past day has been so full of troubles
　I can barely take in this miracle.
　I dread some obstacle to your kindness.
　The court changes its course so easily –
　and fear always mingles with a great love.

Agrippina
   Yes, but then I spoke and everything changed.
   My involvement leaves no room for your doubts:
   I can guarantee a peace I have forged
   with my hands – Nero gave me certain proof.
   If you'd only seen with what tenderness
   he renewed his pledges and promises.
   He stopped me just now and hugged me tightly.
   As we parted his arms held on to me.
   An open kindness bathed his forehead.
   He revealed his deepest secrets to me.
   He poured himself out like a true son who
   in freedom seeks solace on his mother's breast –
   but soon, putting back on his austere mask
   he spoke like an emperor, consulting me,
   his mother, and he then placed in my hands
   secrets on which human lives were hanging.
   No, let it now be said to his renown
   there is no secret darkness in his heart.
   Only our enemies changed his kindness –
   took advantage of some weakness of his.
   But their power is at last on the wane
   and Rome will once more fear Agrippina.
   Already they're celebrating my hold –
   But let's not stand here until the night falls,
   let's share with Octavia the happy end
   of a day that I feared would prove fateful.
   But what do I hear, what's this confusion?
   What is it?

Junia
   Heavens, save Britannicus!

SCENE FOUR

Agrippina, Junia, Burrhus.

Agrippina
Burrhus, where are you going, stop, what is –?

Burrhus
It's done. Britannicus is dying – now –

Junia
My prince!

Agrippina
Dying?

Burrhus
– or rather he is dead.

Junia
I'll save him and if I can't, follow him.

SCENE FIVE

Agrippina, Burrhus.

Agrippina
What a crime, Burrhus.

Burrhus
I won't survive it.
It is time to leave Nero and the court.

Agrippina
He felt no horror of his brother's blood?

Burrhus
His act was more subtle and indirect.
As soon as the Emperor saw his brother

63

he rose, he embraced him, there was silence.
And then Nero takes a cup in his hands.
'So that this day can end auspiciously,'
he says, 'I now sprinkle this libation
and I call upon the gods for success,
let them favour our reconciliation.'
Britannicus swears in the same manner.
The cup he holds is filled by Narcissus –
but as soon as his lips touch the rim
the light escapes from his eyes – he falls down –
the sword's might doesn't compare – without life.
Imagine what this does to those watching:
half leave screaming but the others, who know
the court, stay, model their faces on Nero's.
Nero remains reclined on his own couch
and betrays neither surprise nor concern,
saying: 'He's suffered from this since childhood.
Fear nothing, he'll recover soon enough.'
Narcissus tries hard to show some unease
but his joy leaks out all over his face.
As for me, at the risk of Nero's wrath
I frayed myself a path through the assembly
and I went out, bowed down by this murder
to weep for Britannicus, Nero, Rome.

Agrippina
Here he is, you'll see if I inspired this –

SCENE SIX

Agrippina, Nero, Burrhus, Narcissus.

Nero
Gods!

Agrippina
Nero, stop – I have this to say to you:

64

Britannicus is dead. I see the blow.
I recognise the murderer.

Nero
Who?

Agrippina
You.

Nero
I? So that's where your suspicions always fall.
It seems there's no baseness I won't commit
and anyone listening to you will soon
believe that it was I who killed Claudius.
You loved his son, it seems you mourn his death,
but I cannot answer for Fate's decree.

Agrippina
Britannicus died from drinking poison.
Narcissus did it but you ordered it.

Nero
Who could possibly have told you such things?

Narcissus
My lord, why should these suspicions harm you?
Dear lady: Britannicus was plotting
things that might have caused you much more grief.
He wished for more than marriage to Junia.
He was deceiving you – his wounded heart
wanted to reclaim his former power.
Perhaps Nero was aware of such threats.
Perhaps he trusted me to save his life.
Either way, let your enemies mourn him
and call it a terrible blow, but you –

Agrippina
Follow this minister's advice, Nero:
you'll soon be known for some glorious deeds.
Follow this path: you won't turn back now.
Your brother's blood is on your hands – how long

before it is the blood of your mother?
In your deepest heart, you hate me, I know.
You have hated this yoke of gratitude,
but don't think I'll release you with my death:
I will not allow you to live in peace.
Rome, this sky, the life I gave you will
surge before you at every moment
and remorse will stalk you like a fury.
You'll try to find solace in other crimes,
but the heavens, one day weary of you,
will add you to the list of your victims.
When you are covered in their blood and mine
you will add your own blood and strike yourself.
And the cruellest tyrants of the future
will shrink before the cruelty you've displayed.
This is the fate my heart foresees for you.
You may leave. Go.

Nero
Narcissus, follow me.

SCENE SEVEN

Agrippina, Burrhus.

Agrippina
Heavens, how unjust were my suspicions.
I trusted Narcissus, condemned Burrhus.
Did you see with what looks Nero left me?
The rage in his eyes, Burrhus, said it all.
This is it. There's nothing to stop him now.
The end I was predicted approaches fast.
He will attack you as well soon enough.

Burrhus
I have lived a day too long anyway.
I would thank the heavens if his cruel hand

tried on me the blows of his new-found rage.
Had he done that I would not be mourning
the certain destruction of this country.
This despair is not only for his crime:
a jealous man could have killed his brother.
But I'll tell you what pains me so: Nero's
face was impassive as his brother died.
His eyes, glazed with indifference, already
have the impervious sheen of a monster
who has been inured to crime since childhood.
Let him finish, let him arrange the death
of an adviser who now can't stand him.
The quickest death would the most welcome.

SCENE EIGHT

Agrippina, Burrhus, Albine.

Albine

Run to the Emperor, save him from himself.

Agrippina

Is it Junia? Has she ended her life?

Albine

She's not dead, but she's dead to Nero.
You knew how quickly she fled from this place.
She pretended to go to Octavia
but instead found passageways and escaped
out of the palace where I saw her rush
first towards the statue of Augustus.
There, shedding tears over the marbled feet
and clinging with all her might, she cried out:
'Prince, protect what's left of your family.
Rome witnessed in this palace the murder
of the one heir who could emulate you.
They want me to betray his memory

but I'll keep the promises I made to him:
I'll devote myself to the gods you've joined –
in the temple which honours your virtue.'
People, surprised, gather from everywhere.
They surround her, protect her, cry for her,
and in one voice pledge their support of her.
They lead her to the temple where virgins
devoted to cult of our gods reside,
faithfully guarding the sacred fires.
Nero sees them go, doesn't dare stop them.
But Narcissus more bold – to please Nero –
runs towards Junia, and with no sense of awe
but with defiled hands, tries to force her back.
A thousand blows punish his rashness
and his profane blood spurts over the girl.
Nero, astounded by what is before him,
abandons the body to the crowd.
He goes back in. All flee his fierce silence.
No word escapes from his lips but 'Junia'.
He walks aimlessly and his shifting eyes
drift here, there, but never towards the heavens.
There's now fear that as the night falls
solitude will aggravate his suffering –
and if you abandon him without help,
that his sorrows will soon cut short his life.
There's no time to lose, hurry, run to him,
the slightest upset will destroy him.

Agrippina

That would be only justice, nothing more.
Let us go and see where his grief takes him.

Burrhus

If only this were the last of his crimes.

The End.